Audio, Video & Presentation Skills
for Churches & Pastors

From one who has been learning how to do it for over 30 years

Michael Harvey Koplitz

Table of Contents

Why is it necessary to create brilliant audio for streaming and recording? 6

Microphone quality... 9

Directional microphones...10

Positioning microphones 15

Using the mixing board for audio input 16

Speakers 17

Sound level 18

Equalizing/Normalizing sound for recordings.............20

How to create high-quality videos..............................22

Resolution: HDMI, 2K, 4K, frame rates 22

Camera quality 29

Resolution 29

Lens/Sensor Size 29

Lens Quality...30

Image Processing..30

Low-Light Performance..30

Autofocus Speed and Accuracy................................30

Dynamic Range 31

Video Capabilities...31

User Interface and Controls 31

Build Quality and Durability 33

Positioning cameras...34

Streaming using OBS..35

Post editing videos Software......................................36

1. Adobe Premiere Pro:..36

2. Final Cut Pro X:..37

3. DaVinci Resolve:...37

4. Sony Vegas Pro:..37

5. iMovie:...38

6. HitFilm Express:...38

7. Lightworks:..38

8. Filmora (Wondershare Filmora):...39

9. Avid Media Composer:...39

10. Camtasia:...39

Filtering Imported Videos 41

Color Correction Filters 41

Color Grading Filters 42

Sepia Tones and Vintage Filters 42

Black and White Filters..42

Contrast Filters:..43

Saturation Filters 43

High Dynamic Range (HDR) Filters:..43

Cross Processing Filters 44

Cool and Warm Filters 44

Cinematic Look Filters 44

Backgrounds and Lighting...46

Graphics: fonts, backgrounds 47

Green Screen 47

Basic Presentation Skills..49

Using a podium...49

Clothing...51

Hands..53

Gestures..54

Moving around while preaching.......................54

Using a script (how to read the sermon with it not looking that way)..56

Eye contact...57

Grammar...57

Lighting...57

Creating a video..59

Recording settings...59

Rendering settings...60

Color schemes..61

Cleaning up a recording.....................................61

Processing voices...62

Using recorded music or videos........................66

Closing Remarks..67

Why is it necessary to create brilliant audio for streaming and recording?

Why is it important to have the highest quality audio and video? Today, people are watching TV shows and movies with 4K brilliance in their homes. The graphics and video effects that are a part of entertainment today are of a quality that the local churches probably will not come too close to. However, the church does not need video effects like Star Wars to communicate the Gospel. There has been an attitude among older members of the church that the worship service is not supposed to be an entertainment. These are the people who object to having projection equipment or TV panels in the sanctuary. Many younger people and older individuals no longer view the use of videos, graphics, and great music as forms of entertainment during worship today.

The idea of only using the old hymns with just an organ or piano is the way to extinction. The growing churches now have multimedia, bands, and semi-professional singers. Large churches even hire personnel who can create multimedia experiences. It has become an expectation. If you are not sure that this is a valid statement, go to a thriving church and sit in on the contemporary worship or whatever term they are using for it. This is the worship service that does not have the organ, usually, and a band instead of a choir.

I am sorry to say that the days of hymns, prayers, and a sermon will not cut it. Now that I have made that statement, keep in mind that Christians, both young and old, still have a fondness for this type of service. Using 300-year-old hymns with King James English may not attract the younger crowd. It is more difficult to attract people who are used to Star Wars graphics and sounds to traditional worship.[1]

---

[1] "Why Men Hate Going to Church" by David Murrow

It is important for the church pastor, staff, and leaders to understand what the next generation of Christians will help them worship God. You may not feel that the contemporary worship style is your cup of tea. However, there are plenty of people who need this new experience. The contemporary worship movement began before the year 2000. It has collected steam and is a part of a growing congregation.

This book is a part of a class on how-to create high-quality multimedia worship. Even if your church is doing traditional worship, there is plenty of information in the book about how to do audio, video, and presentation skills. This book has ideas and some instructions on how to do things. The class will show how to establish and create multimedia worship.

Microphone quality

This is the key to voice audio. Churches tend to purchase the least expensive microphones they can get. Inexpensive is equivalent to low quality. The first thing to look at when selecting a microphone is the response range.

The typical hearing range for humans is from 20 Hz to 20,000 Hz (20 kHz). This range represents the frequencies that the average human ear can perceive. However, individual variations can occur, and factors such as age, exposure to loud noises, and other health-related issues can affect an individual's hearing range.

As people age, their ability to hear higher frequencies may diminish, a condition known as presbycusis. Younger individuals, especially children and teenagers, often have a broader hearing range compared to older adults.

Therefore, do not purchase a microphone that is outside this range. The second thing is to discover what the range of your equipment is. If your mixing board can only handle sound between 100 and 18,000 hz, then you either have to upgrade the mixing board or you can purchase a microphone with a range matching the board. Then you must consider the speaker range and if you use an amplifier, its range.

The best audio will be when all the equipment is at the range 20 to 20,000 hz. Everyone in the congregation will hear all the sounds that a band, a person, or video can produce.

Directional microphones

A unidirectional microphone, also known as a directional microphone, collects sound predominantly from one direction. Engineers design these microphones to focus on capturing audio from a specific source while minimizing background noise and sounds coming from other directions. Users commonly use unidirectional microphones in various applications where isolating sound from a particular direction is essential.

There are two main types of unidirectional microphones:

1. Cardioid Microphones: These microphones have a heart-shaped pickup pattern, with maximum sensitivity to sound coming from the front and sides and reduced sensitivity to sounds coming from the rear. The term "cardioid" refers to the shape of the microphone's pickup pattern.

2. Supercardioid and Hypercardioid Microphones: These microphones have narrower pickup patterns than cardioid microphones, providing even greater directionality. Supercardioid and hypercardioid microphones are often used in situations where precise control over the pickup direction is crucial,

such as in film production or on-stage performances.

Unidirectional microphones are favored in environments where there is potential for background noise or where the sound source is localized, as they help to isolate the desired audio and rejecting unwanted noise from other directions. This makes them suitable for applications such as live performances, recording studios, broadcasting, public speaking, and field recording.

Some microphones use phantom power. This is a low power circuit that comes from the mixer board to power the microphone. Higher end mixers will have phantom power for the microphones. Therefore, if you have a phantom microphone connected to a mixer with it and the microphone does not work, the first step in troubleshooting is to make sure the phantom power is on (I have experienced this problem).

Shure microphones are the best (that is my opinion). You will see podcasters using Shure microphones. The Shure SM7B microphone[2] is what I use for my radio show recordings. It is a unidirectional microphone that does not collect background sounds unless they are loud. Of course, the speaker needs to be close to the microphone when using it (I call it eating the microphone. Watch a video of professional singers and you will see what I mean).

You will need a different type of microphone if you want to capture the sound of a choir, or a group of people in a band. If you want to capture the voice of the band members, it is best to get a high end microphone for each member of the band. It is important for high audio quality to purchase high end microphones.

---

[2] Amazon.com: Shure SM7B Dynamic Vocal Microphone : Musical Instruments

When purchasing a high end microphone you will need to get a high end cable. This would be a cable that is shielded. You will need to check the distance from the microphone to the mixing board. You may need boosters. The audio signal experiences a greater decibel loss as the cable gets longer. The specifications of the microphone will tell you what the maximum distance that you can run a cable with little signal loss. The more the signal loss, the more the audio signal will degrade.

The cable booster will have to be determined by the overall distance between the microphone and the mixer board.

Positioning microphones

The closer the person is to the microphone, the better the audio. Sometimes, people use a voice screen in front of the microphone. This is to soften the "p," "b," and "t" sounds.

When capturing sound from a group, like a choir, one should use and place a bidirectional or multidirectional microphone over the heads of the group.

Wireless microphones are nice because they do not have a cable and the person using the wireless microphone can move. Before purchasing such a microphone, it is important to discover the range of the transmitter. Also, a consideration is how close the church is to another church using wireless microphones. There is the possibility that one wireless microphone can interfere with another. When this happens, it is important that the wireless microphone purchased has multiple channels. Keep the receiver for the microphone away from Wi-Fi modems and any other equipment that transmits a signal. This will reduce the chance of having interference.

Shure has high-quality wireless microphones. Make sure that the wireless microphone, transmitter, and receiver work together to ensure high-quality audio is received.

Using the mixing board for audio input

The mixing board can send your audio output to an amplifier or a streaming device (i.e. computer). If the mixer board has an amplifier, the outputs from the mixer board can go directly to the speakers. It is best to use shielded cables from the mixer board or the amplifier to the speakers or even to the streaming device.

Speakers

The speakers must be able to handle the audio range of the equipment. The placement of the speakers is determined by the sanctuary or the room that it is being placed in. However, Bosse manufactures a tower speaker that can be placed in the corner of a room and can broadcast sound to the entire room. Before permanently placing speakers, it is wise to take a decibel meter and ensure that the same decibel level is throughout the room. Naturally, when you are closer to the speakers, the decibel level will be higher. A change of 5 dB is within accepted limits.

However, make sure that the person(s) who are doing the sound have a good range of hearing. I should highlight that the person running your sound board (the mixer) must be able to hear the range of sounds that your system can produce. I have been in churches where the sound engineer at the mixer board is hard of hearing. The sound in the room or sanctuary will suffer.

Also, placing the mixer board is essential. Usually, the best place is the rear of the sanctuary or room and in the middle. Too many churches place the mixer board in a corner. In one church there was a 10 dB drop in sound from the middle of the sanctuary to the back left corner where the mixer board and sound engineer sat. This is not a good idea.

Sound level

People typically measure sound levels in units called decibels (dB). The decibel scale is logarithmic, meaning that each increase of 10 dB represents a tenfold increase in sound intensity. Here are some common sound levels and their corresponding descriptions:

1. 0 dB: The threshold of human hearing.

2. 10 dB: Rustling leaves.

3. 20 dB: Whispering.

4. 30 dB: Quiet library.

5. 40 dB: Quiet residential area at night.

6. 50 dB: Light traffic or a quiet office.

7. 60 dB: Normal conversation.

8. 70 dB: Vacuum cleaner or busy traffic.

9. 80 dB: Garbage disposal or busy street noise.

10. 90 dB: Lawn mower or subway train.

11. 100 dB: Chainsaw or a loud concert.

12. 110 dB: Car horn or rock concert.

13. 120 dB: Thunder or a jet taking off.

14. 130 dB: Threshold of pain, potential hearing damage.

15. 140 dB and above: Gunshots, fireworks, or other extremely loud noises, high risk of hearing damage.

It's important to note that prolonged exposure to sounds above 85 dB can lead to hearing damage or loss. It is important to note that individuals should wear hearing protection in environments where the sound levels consistently exceed safe limits. Keep in mind that the perception of loudness can vary from person to person, and factors such as frequency and duration of exposure also play a role in the potential impact on hearing.

Equalizing/Normalizing sound for recordings

When equalizing sound, we make the decibels for each section of sound, the Hz, equal. An equalizer device, or software is used to bring the various Hz levels equal. Therefore, the bass, treble and midrange sounds are at the same decibel level.

When making a recording, you can normalize the entire sound clip. This process is to ensure that there are overwhelming sounds. For example, normalizing a sound clip to let's say 6 dB means that no sound will exceed that amount. When putting multiple videos together, normalizing the sound ensures that the volume does not need to be adjusted when playing back the clips.

How to create high-quality videos

High-quality videos depend on the quality of the camera. Today, many smart phones have a camera. Some have top quality cameras. They will take good videos. The problem with smartphones is that the lens is small. This will not allow for as much light for the capturing of the images. A larger lens will allow for more light to be captured, thus giving a higher quality video. Cameras with high-quality large lenses are used to film TV shows and movies.

A smartphone or even a PC webcam will create a video. However, it will not be the best quality. It cannot capture all the details.

Resolution: HDMI, 2K, 4K, frame rates

Video resolution refers to the number of distinct pixels that can be displayed in each dimension of a video image. It is a key factor in determining the clarity and sharpness of a video. Resolution is typically expressed as the width x height of the image in pixels. For example, a video with a resolution of 1920 x 1080 means it has a width of 1920 pixels and a height of 1080 pixels.

Common video resolutions include:

1. SD (Standard Definition):
   - 640 x 480 pixels (480p)
   - 720 x 480 pixels (DVD resolution)

2. HD (High Definition):
   - 1280 x 720 pixels (720p)
   - 1920 x 1080 pixels (1080p)

3. Full HD:
   - 1920 x 1080 pixels (1080p)

4. 2K:
   - 2048 x 1080 pixels

5. Ultra HD (UHD) or 4K:

   - 3840 x 2160 pixels (2160p)

6. 8K:

   - 7680 x 4320 pixels

Higher resolutions provide more detail and clarity, especially on larger screens. However, the actual perceived improvement in quality depends on factors such as screen size, viewing distance, and individual visual acuity.

It's important to note that higher resolution videos also require more storage space and processing power. The content must be recorded, edited, and displayed on devices that support the respective resolution for viewers to experience the increased detail.

As technology evolves, higher resolutions like 8K and beyond continue to emerge, offering even greater levels of detail for those with compatible display devices.

Now, let's discuss the downside of resolutions. The captured image file will grow with the higher resolution. Therefore, one ensures a camera has a large enough memory capacity if higher resolutions are used. Of course, the length of the video will cause the file to grow.

There are options to compress video when taking it. This will reduce the file size however, compressing a video takes processing time away from the camera. If possible, it is best to avoid using compression when taking a video. Compression can be added when the video is processed.

Video frame rate, measured in frames per second (fps), refers to the number of individual frames or images displayed in one second of video playback. It is a crucial parameter in determining the smoothness and fluidity of motion in a video. The frame rate is an essential aspect of video production and playback, impacting the viewing experience.

Common video frame rates include:

1. 24 fps (frames per second): Commonly used in film production. It has a cinematic look and is often referred to as "24p."

2. 30 fps: Commonly used in North America for television and online video content. It provides a smoother motion than 24 fps.

3. 60 fps: Provides even smoother motion than 30 fps and is commonly used for video games, high-speed action footage, and some online video content.

4. 120 fps, 240 fps, etc.: Higher frame rates are often used for slow-motion footage. For example, if recorded at 120 fps and played back at 30 fps, the video will appear in slow motion.

5. 50 fps and 25 fps: Commonly used in PAL regions (Europe, Asia, Australia) for television and video production.

6. 29.97 fps: Used in North America for television to accommodate the NTSC video standard. It is derived from the original 30 fps standard.

The choice of frame rate depends on the type of content, the desired visual effect, and the standards or preferences of the platform on which the video will be displayed. For example, cinematic productions often use 24 fps for its traditional filmic appearance, while higher frame rates are common in sports broadcasts and action-packed video games to capture fast-paced motion more smoothly.

The frame rate, when combined with the video resolution, affects the overall data size of the video file. Higher frame rates may cause larger file sizes. Not all display devices or platforms support all frame rates, so compatibility is a consideration when producing and distributing video content.

Camera quality

The term "camera quality" encompasses several aspects that contribute to the overall performance and capability of a camera. Different cameras, such as those found in smartphones, digital cameras, or professional DSLRs, may prioritize certain features. Here are key factors that contribute to camera quality.

Resolution

Resolution in megapixels (MP) is measured by digital cameras. Higher megapixel counts allow for sharper and more detailed images.

Lens/Sensor Size

A larger sensor typically captures more light, resulting in better low-light performance and improved image quality. Common sensor sizes include full-frame, APS-C, and micro four-thirds.

Lens Quality

The quality of the lens plays a crucial role in image sharpness, clarity, and overall optical performance. Higher-end cameras often allow for interchangeable lenses, offering greater flexibility.

Image Processing

The image processing capabilities of a camera have an influence on the accuracy of colors, the dynamic range, and the overall appearance of the images. Advanced image processors can enhance image quality and reduce noise.

Low-Light Performance

Cameras with better low-light performance can capture clear and detailed images in challenging lighting conditions. Sensor size, aperture size, and image processing influences this.

Autofocus Speed and Accuracy

Fast and accurate autofocus is essential for capturing sharp images, especially in dynamic or fast-paced situations. Phase-detection and contrast-detection are common autofocus methods.

Dynamic Range

Dynamic range refers to the camera's ability to capture details in both bright highlights and dark shadows. Cameras with higher dynamic range can produce more balanced and visually appealing images.

Video Capabilities

For cameras capable of recording video, factors such as resolution, frame rate, and additional features like image stabilization and autofocus during video recording contribute to overall video quality.

User Interface and Controls

A user interface that is well-designed and controls that are intuitive can make it easier for photographers to access and adjust settings, thus enhancing their overall experience.

Build Quality and Durability

The physical construction of the camera, including the materials used, weather sealing, and overall build quality, can affect its longevity and ability to withstand various conditions.

It's important to note that the concept of "camera quality" can be subjective and depends on the specific needs and preferences of the user. The best camera for a particular individual will depend on their intended use, whether it's casual photography, professional work, or specific requirements such as portability or versatility.

Positioning cameras

The best position of the camera is at eye level with the person being videoed. To capture the congregation, the camera must be placed high enough to be a foot or so above the tallest person. Therefore, seven feet is usually a respectful distance.

Streaming using OBS

OBS is a software package that is free on Windows and Mac. Users can use OBS for streaming and recording. The beauty of OBS is that you can have multiple audio and video inputs. You can also place graphics on the canvas. OBS also has scenes capabilities, and it is easy for the person running the video to switch between scenes.

Therefore, OBS allows the video engineer to determine which camera to use (in a multi-camera environment) and can have multiple audio inputs. OBS will also allow for recording and streaming at the same time. It has a virtual camera capability which allows for streaming to social media. OBS would control the control of cameras and audio. The virtual camera option would then transmit the video and audio streams.

Post editing videos Software

Post editing videos can be done with any video processing software package.

There are many video processing software packages available, catering to different needs, ranging from basic video editing to advanced post-production tasks. Here are some popular video processing software packages:

1. Adobe Premiere Pro:
This professional video editing software is widely used in the film and television industry. It offers a comprehensive set of tools for video editing, color correction, audio editing, and more.

2. Final Cut Pro X:

A professional video editing software designed for Mac users. It provides advanced features for video editing, color grading, and audio editing, with a focus on efficiency and performance.

3. DaVinci Resolve:

Known for its powerful color correction and grading capabilities, DaVinci Resolve also includes advanced video editing and audio post-production features. It's available in both free and paid versions.

4. Sony Vegas Pro:

A video editing software that caters to both beginners and professionals. It offers a range of features, including multi-camera editing, 3D editing, and advanced audio tools.

5. iMovie:

Apple's video editing software designed for macOS and iOS users. iMovie is user-friendly and suitable for basic video editing needs, making it a good choice for beginners.

6. HitFilm Express:

A free video editing and visual effects software with a wide range of features. It includes advanced video editing tools, compositing, and 3D effects.

7. Lightworks:

A professional-grade video editing software available in both free and paid versions. It has been used in the editing of numerous well-known films.

8. Filmora (Wondershare Filmora):

A user-friendly video editing software suitable for beginners. It provides a range of creative tools and effects for video editing.

9. Avid Media Composer:

Widely used in the film and broadcast industry, Avid Media Composer is a professional video editing software with advanced features and collaborative tools.

10. Camtasia:

Screen recording and video editing software is often used for creating tutorials, presentations, and educational content. It's user-friendly and suitable for beginners.

When selecting video processing software, you should take into consideration factors such as your skill level, specific editing requirements, platform compatibility (Windows, macOS, or Linux), and budget. Many software packages offer free trials, allowing you to explore their features before making a purchase. The choice may depend on whether you need basic editing, advanced post-production features, or specialized tools for tasks like color grading or visual effects.

Filtering Imported Videos

When importing a video into any of these products, consider using the SHARP, and CONTRAST filters. In addition, use a color filter to enhance your video image.

Video color filters, often referred to as video color grading or filters, are tools used to adjust and enhance the colors in a video. They play a significant role in setting the mood, tone, and overall visual style of a video. Here are some common types of video color filters and their purposes:

Color Correction Filters

Corrective filters are used to fix color issues in the footage. This includes adjusting white balance to ensure accurate color representation and correcting color imbalances caused by different lighting conditions.

Color Grading Filters

Grading filters apply to create a specific look or style for the video. This can involve adjusting the overall color tone, adding color tints, or creating a particular atmosphere that aligns with the video's narrative or genre.

Sepia Tones and Vintage Filters

These filters give a video of an aged or nostalgic look by applying a brownish or yellowish tint. They are often used to evoke a sense of history or warmth.

Black and White Filters

Converting a video to black and white can add a classic and timeless feel. Artists or filmmakers often use it for artistic or dramatic effect.

Contrast Filters:

Adjusting contrast can impact the visual dynamics of a video. Increasing contrast makes the colors more vibrant and distinct, while reducing contrast can create a softer, more muted appearance.

Saturation Filters

Saturation filters control the intensity of colors in a video. Increasing saturation enhances vibrancy, while reducing saturation can create a more muted or desaturated look.

High Dynamic Range (HDR) Filters:

HDR filters aim to expand the dynamic range of a video, enhancing details in both the shadows and highlights. HDR can provide a more lifelike and visually appealing image.

Cross Processing Filters

Cross processing mimics the effects of using unconventional film development techniques. It results in unique color shifts and contrasts, often producing a stylized and artistic look.

Cool and Warm Filters

Cool tones (blues and greens) and warm tones (reds and yellows) can be applied to convey specific emotions or enhance the mood of a scene.

Cinematic Look Filters

Filters are designed to replicate the color grading styles commonly seen in films, adding a cinematic quality to the video.

Many video editing software applications provide a range of built-in color filters, and professional color grading software offers even more advanced options. The choice of color filters depends on the creative vision of the video producer and the desired impact on the audience. Experimenting with different filters can help achieve a unique and visually interesting look for a video.

Backgrounds and Lighting

This section is about when you have control of the background and or lighting. Let us say that you are recording yourself in an office. The pictures on the wall, the lighting of the room, the windows, can all make a difference in the video's quality. For example, if a picture is behind you and the light from the window creates a glare on the picture, then it will show up on the video.

The best lighting is to have the light source in front of you at eye level. You may have to turn up or down the panel slightly so that the panel does not blind you.

The worst light source will be one that is directly overhead. The light will glare off the top of your head. The best white light is 5000 kelvins. This is equivalent to sunlight. Using different kelvin amounts will allow for dimmer or brighter videos. Use different kelvin values in your videos to get different moods.

Graphics: fonts, backgrounds

The optimal graphic for words is a black background with white letters of at least 24 points. Ariel is a good font for words. A display can show responsive readings to assist the congregation. Hymn and song verses being displayed are also a great help. For example, on Christmas Eve during the candle lighting ritual, it is difficult to hold a lit candle and a hymnal. Having the words to the song on a screen is helpful. I was told that a person holding a baby also finds it beneficial to have the words of the song or hymn on a screen.

Green Screen

Using a green screen is nice because it will allow you to change out the green screen for pictures or video. The lighting on the green screen must be placed so that shadows do not appear on the green screen when you are in front of it. That will require multiple light sources. Having a green screen without creases in it is best. If you use two or more green screens, ensure they are of the same color. Then make sure you have no green clothing on. If you do, when you key out the green screen, you will find holes in yourself. If you want to have holes in your image, then wear green. There are some fun YouTube videos of people wearing green clothes. Meteorologists have made this mistake the most.

Basic Presentation Skills

It is great to create a wonderful and powerful sermon, but without excellent presentation skills, the true value of the message may not occur. Unfortunately, seminaries do not teach presentation skills to potential preachers. The items mentioned here will help in preaching and teaching.

Using a podium

A podium places a barrier between the speaker and the congregation or class members. In various churches, the congregation requires the preacher to remain behind it. I was told by a church member that what I said was not a sermon if I moved away from the podium. The problem with a podium is that the preacher is not moving. It is more difficult to focus on a preacher who is not moving than one who is. As a preacher, if I can move, I must either memorize the sermon or follow an outline and create it spontaneously. Of course, the preacher should create a sermon and know what the contents are being attempting to go without a script. It takes a lot of practice to leave the notes behind.

If you have never left the podium and want to, a suggestion is to do 85% of the sermon at the podium with your notes or full sermon. Then, for the last part, walk away from the podium and freehand it. Over time, the freehand will become longer and longer. It takes a lot of confidence to move away from the podium. There are very few pastors who do.

When you leave the podium, do not stand in the same place too long. Moving around slowly will cause the congregation to move their heads to see you. It will keep them engaged. Using hand gestures and facial expressions are a part of the move. Yes, employ facial gestures and hand movements at the podium. It is also not common for preachers to use them at podiums. Using your voice and movements helps in keeping the listeners' attention.

Many preachers will grasp the podium when not turning pages. This is a sign that the preacher is nervous. People will see this and sense the situation. They will become concerned about the preacher's welfare and will not hear the message.

If you are a guest preacher or teacher and you are going to use the podium, allow the people to see all of you for approximately 15 seconds before moving behind it. It is a good time to introduce yourself. People want to know what you look like. A problem during Covid was facemasks. When the speaker's face cannot be seen, it becomes a mystery to the listener and a distraction.

Clothing

For men, it is easy. It is up to the congregation how dressed up the male preacher needs to be. I am sorry to write this for the ladies, but I was told this in a presentation skills class I took in the early 1990s and I have added it to every presentation skills class I have facilitated. A lady's outfit will cause a judgment from the men and women in the congregation. If the outfit is tight fitting, it can be a distraction. Wearing short dresses or skirts will cause the men to stray from your message. Sorry ladies to say this, but I think you get the idea of what I am saying. This is where church robes are useful.

Avoid the color brown, especially dark brown. This is considered a boring color. Also, avoid bright pastels because they are distracting. Color coordination is important and if you are like me, I wore white shirts with every suit or jacket and pant combination to the worship service. The jacket and pants had the same color. It made my color coordination easy.

For the men wearing ties with pictures and decorative designs might look nice, but they can be distracting. Even for the men, a church robe can be a friend.

Hands

Whether you are preaching or teaching, your hand placement is important. Keep your hands out of your pockets. If there are keys or coins in the pocket, there is a tendency to jiggle them. That is very distracting, and you will lose the congregation to that sound. If you are behind the podium, I mentioned your hands should not cling to it. Placing your hands on the podium is fine. Hand movement is good to do because it gets the listener to move their eyes and stay in focus. It is hard to zone out when you are watching someone move, even if it is a little bit.

When you are in front of the group, and you do not have a hand gesture in mind, the best place for your hands is found by imagining a triangle from your belly button to your waist with the ends at your hips. That is the best place for hands when not gesturing.

Gestures

There are obvious gestures that you definitely do not want to use. I am sure you know them. Other hand and arm movements are acceptable. There are people who talk with their hands. Too many hand gestures are distracting. No hand gestures will put the listeners to sleep. Find a happy medium.

Moving around while preaching

We have already reviewed this. One thing to avoid is to move into the congregation or class unless you want to make a point. All eyes will be upon you if you move up the aisle. Sometimes it is a good thing, but it can easily backfire. You must know your congregation or class members before doing it.

Movement in front of the church or classroom will work to keep the listeners' attention on you.

Using a script (how to read the sermon with it not looking that way)

Almost all preachers use a script. The problem with a script is that it is usually corrected grammatically. We do not talk with perfect grammar. Therefore, I highly suggest that you dictate your sermon into your computer or device. Then, when you correct it, leave some of the incorrect grammar in place. If you correct all the grammar, then your sermon comes across as being read. With some bad grammar, the sermon will be heard in conversational mode.

You will need to look up as much as possible. If it is possible to have a stand with the document on it at a 45 degree angle, then you can look at the paper and still appear to be looking at the congregation. Here's a trick I collected over the years. If you look at the people in the third row of the church, everyone will think that you are looking at them. In various churches, the first row or two are empty, anyway.

Eye contact

The eye trick explained above is good to know. Don't forget to move your eyes to each side occasionally unless you only have people in the middle of the sanctuary or room. That rarely happens. This additional movement will give the impression that you are looking at everyone in the sanctuary or room.

Grammar

I mentioned the use of grammar to change the idea of having an academic read paper. If there are idioms used in regular conversation, then use them.

Lighting

We have discussed most of the lighting techniques. There are some church sanctuaries that will not allow you to adjust the lighting. In that case, you must make the best of things. Some problems with bad lighting can be adjusted in post processing. Remember, the better the lighting, the better the video image.

Creating a video

Recording settings

When you are creating a video, you must determine who your audience is and whether this is a temporary video or a permanent video. For example, when I create a worship by subject video, I consider this to be temporary or possibly it's better to say somewhat informal. Therefore, I do not break out the green screen. However, for my educational videos, I use the green screen. If you are going to place graphics and/or text on your video, it may be wise to use a green screen so that you can have a nice clean background.

Determine what your resolution will be for your final video output, and it is wise then to create the same video output on your camera. Always use the highest audio settings that your camera recording device will allow.

I recommend you do not use a Bluetooth microphone, specially connected to a PC, because you may get skips in your video. I have used a Bluetooth microphone in the past and found the skips difficult to discover where they came from. Then I realized it was the Bluetooth microphone cutting in and out. Therefore, I do not use a Bluetooth microphone for educational videos.

Rendering settings

These settings are determined by what you want your output to be. Depending on the software you are using to do rendering, you will probably have several presets. I have found that if I use H.264, every social media device and YouTube have no problem with it. It also depends on whether you are going to compress your video. Because when you are compressing your video, your output may not matter as much. However, you want to ensure that you are going to have the resolution in the frame rates you need for the video, as described earlier in the book.

Color schemes

Color schemes are called LUTS in the rendering world. You can find on the Internet a lot of free LUTS. These are presets for your color and your exposure when you are processing your video. As the editor, determine which color configuration you wish to use. Remember, your camera may have a filter already built into it. For example, the iPhone can be programmed to give you color filtering. It is recommended that you do not use any filtering when making your recording and then when you process your video, you can determine what color scheme you want to use.

Cleaning up a recording

When you import your video into your video processing software, you will want to consider adding a SHARP effect to the video. This will bring out the details in the video. Be careful not to add too much SHARP because it will look a little odd. The best thing is to play with the sharp effect and see if you like it. You can also add an effect which will negate any key stoning that your camera lens has. Whether you get a convex or concave video output, which will allow you to flatten your video. For example, if you use a 28 mm fisheye lens, you can see the curvature of your video. By using a filter in the video processing software, you can flatten that video out, so it does not look as "fisheyed."

Processing voices

There have been some great enhancements to clean up voices. In Adobe Premiere Pro release 24.2, you can enhance the voice of your speaker on your video. You can also give your voice the effect of being in a large room, or a small room, or any kind of room. Add these sound effects to your video and determine which is the best to use.

The range of the human voice refers to pitches or frequencies that a person can produce with their vocal cords. The human vocal range is typically divided into different vocal registers, each covering a specific range of pitches. The three main registers are:

1. Chest voice: This is the lower range of the voice, produced with the chest muscles. It is often associated with speaking and lower musical notes.

2. Head voice: This is the higher range of the voice, produced with the head resonators. It is commonly used for higher pitches in singing.

3. Falsetto: This is an even higher range than the head voice and is produced by vibrating only the edges of the vocal cords. It is often used for very high-pitched singing.

The overall vocal range varies from person to person and is influenced by factors such as age, gender, and vocal training. The average adult male has a vocal range of about an octave and a half to two octaves, while the average adult female has a range of about two to three octaves. However, there are individuals with larger or smaller vocal ranges depending on their unique physiological characteristics and training. Professional singers, especially those who have undergone vocal training, may have an extended range.

The typical frequency range of the human voice spans from approximately 80 Hz to 1100 Hz. This range covers the fundamental frequencies of most vocal sounds. Keep in mind that these values are general estimates, and individual variations can occur.

Bass frequencies (chest voice): The lower frequencies, associated with the chest voice in singing and lower-pitched speech, range from approximately 80 Hz to 250 Hz.

Midrange frequencies (modal voice): The modal voice, used in normal speaking and singing, falls within the range of about 250 Hz to 800 Hz.

Treble frequencies (head voice and falsetto): Higher frequencies, associated with the head voice and falsetto in singing, can extend from around 800 Hz to 1100 Hz and beyond.

These frequency ranges are approximate and can vary among individuals. Professional singers, especially those with training, may have a broader range and can reach higher frequencies. The human voice produces harmonics and overtones that contribute to its overall sound, adding complexity to the frequency spectrum.

Using recorded music or videos

Be careful when using recorded music because of copyright laws. The music I use in my worship videos I purchased from Iworship. Therefore, in this case, I am free to use these videos. If you download videos from YouTube, they are usually fine to use. However, if you place your output on YouTube, you may get a notification that a copyright is involved. Make sure that you do not go over three strikes on copyright because if you do, they will cancel your account. Usually, your video will be blocked in certain countries because of some copyright violation, which may or may not be a true violation, or YouTube will not allow you to monetize the video.

Closing Remarks

I will admit at the creation of this book, I cannot be certain that I covered all the topics that you may be interested in. Feel free to contact me through my author's page on amazon.com or at my personal website (http://michaelkoplitz.info). On my website, you can access all the videos that I have posted on the Internet, including the educational ones. Hopefully, this will give you a feeling of what I have been doing.

Remember that the hardest is video to record is the one in the sanctuary because you are usually limited to where you can place your cameras. The audio will be best if you can connect to the soundboard, but numerous times that is difficult and you will have to rely on the sound that comes to your camera. If you have to use the camera microphone then consider placing two or more microphones strategically in the church where the highest decibel rating is. You can usually download an app for your smart phone which will detect the decibel levels. Remember that your decibel level is going to change throughout your worship because an organ with the congregation singing is going to have a higher decibel level than when you are speaking.

The most important thing is to have fun making videos. I am sure to some of you it sounds like a chore, but over time it becomes fun. There are numerous filters, functions and effects that exist in Premier Pro, for example, that I will probably never use them all. There are numerous websites that you can visit where you can buy templates and effects which will enhance your videos. Remember, if you are starting out fresh, your videos are going to improve. You will have an eye for good video and good graphics.

I wish you all the best in your learning and your producing. May the Lord be with you in your work for Him.